LOOKING BACK AT
Rusholme & Fallowfield

Gay Sussex & Peter Helm

Willow PUBLISHING

Willow Pubilshing 1984
Willow Cottage, 36 Moss Lane,
Timperley, Altrincham,
Cheshire, WA15 6SZ

© Peter Helm & Gay Sussex 1984
Reprinted 1991

ISBN 0 946361 10 X

Printed by The Commercial
Centre Ltd., Clowes Street
Hollinwood, Oldham

Contents   page

The 1893 F.A. Cup Final at Fallowfield (behind Owens Park) *right*

It was between Wolverhampton Wanderers and Everton, and Wolves won 1–0. This is the only occasion on which the F.A. Cup Final has been played in Manchester, and the honour belongs to Fallowfield. (The Cup Final has also been played, or replayed, three times at Old Trafford, but of course Old Trafford is not in Manchester.)

Foreword

Other books have been written about the Rusholme and Fallowfield area; there is a list which includes them at the end of this book. Royle's book on Rusholme and Mrs. Williamson's Sketches of Fallowfield are particularly enjoyable, and we hope that, after reading this book, you will want to read further.

We must point out that this book is written around a collection of photographs; it is not intended to be a complete history. Our aim is to give a flavour of the area's past, not a full account. The theme of the book is "Looking Back At", so photographs that show streets and buildings as they are today have not been included.

Many people have helped. Our families have had to put up with requests for more coffee and quiet for many months, so thanks to Graham Sussex, Rachael Sussex, Jasmine Sussex, and especially Dorothy Helm whose knowledge of the area and typing skills, were both appreciated and made full use of.

Also thanks to the various departments of Manchester's Central Library – Local History, Archives, Arts, Social Sciences, and Photographic – to Mrs. Pat Hodson of the Lancashire Bibliography who provided a lot of handy references; the City of Manchester Planning Department; Birch Community Centre, and the Manchester High School for Girls' library. All helped immeasurably with our researches.

The photographs are the main feature of this book and we are very grateful to the following people and organizations for permission to use their photographs – the Local History Library, the Manchester Studies Unit at Manchester Polytechnic, the Greater Manchester Police Museum, the Manchester Transport Museum, the Rusholme and Fallowfield Civic Society, Chris Makepeace, Dr. Bradfield, Mrs. T. Williams, Mrs. Ingham, Mrs. McCluckie, Mr. E. Barrett, and Mrs.I. Mosley.

Fellow members of the Rusholme and Fallowfield Civic Society deserve a special mention. It was their suggestion that we write this book, and their interest in the project and enthusiasm for and knowledge of the neighbourhood was a constant encouragement.

Finally, our apologies for any mistakes and omissions. We have done our best to produce an interesting account of an area for which we both have much affection.

Peter Helm and Gay Sussex, 1984.

Introduction

Rusholme and Fallowfield – the area means different things to different people. To some it's a jumble of streets and shops briefly glimpsed during the peak hour rush; others remember student parties and looming exams. For newcomers from the Sub-Continent, it is often a place of hard work and long hours to establish a shop or restaurant. Some people have lived here for decades and seen many changes, for others it's their first home – knee-deep in stripped pine and pieces of Victoriana, which previous occupants probably would have discarded as being old-fashioned. But, from whatever position you view this area, its story can be absorbing.

Over the years the boundaries of Rusholme and Fallowfield have changed, and it is difficult to be precise about what we mean by Rusholme or Fallowfield. For the purposes of this book, we include Wilmslow Road and the areas on either side of it, from Moss Lane East down to Mauldeth Road.

Rusholme

The early history of Rusholme and Fallowfield is largely hidden from us; and what we do know is nearly all derived from old documents in the archives of the landed families – the Platts, the Birches, and the Worsleys. The working population had little to leave behind it, except apprentice indentures and, occasionally, legal documents relating to disputes.

The earliest evidence that Rusholme was known to man in Roman times was provided by the discovery of about 200 Roman coins of the 3rd and 4th centuries A.D. in a single hoard from a site where, nowadays, the Gore Brook crosses Birchfields Road. This period, towards the end of the Roman occupation, was one of insecurity for the Anglo-Roman population, and the hiding of valuables would be an indication of troubled times. The coins themselves remained hidden until the 1890's, when they were discovered by

Platt Lane, from Taylor Street, 1909

This photograph of Platt Lane, looking towards Wilmslow Road, gives an idea of how Rusholme's residential streets appeared at the turn of the century. The photograph shows the since-demolished outbuildings of Platt Hall, which housed Platt Day Schools from the early fifties until 1861. Fifty years later, when the buildings were about to be demolished, Royle found that the schoolroom and desks were just as they had been left when the school closed! On the left-hand side, the garden wall of Melbourne House can be seen.

workmen, and eventually deposited in the Manchester Museum. One of the coins is in the local history display at the Fletcher Moss branch Art Gallery.

About 800 years after the coins had been in circulation, Rusholme begins to appear in legal documents, the name being variously spelt Russum (1235), Rysshome (1563), and Rushulme (1649). An early deed describing the boundaries of the Platt Estate mentions the Nico Ditch. Its name is spelt in many different ways in deeds, but all the spellings appear to be variations on the word "Mickle", meaning Great. It was undoubtedly a great defensive work, built in troubled times. This Ditch and the nearby Gore Brook have probably been the inspiration behind the stories of battles between the Danes (Danes Road) and the Normans (Norman Road), the dead from which were said to have been buried under Dead Entry (the narrow entry joining Norman Road and Wallace Avenue). But there is no evidence to support these stories, and, certainly Norman Road

was on Platt Estate land, and was named after the family a member of which (Miss Elizabeth Norman, of Winster in Derbyshire) married one of the Worsleys of Platt.

Platt Hall – not the present 18th century building, but its black and white predecessor – was demolished in the mid-eighteenth century, and no pictures of it are known, although a most interesting inventory of its contents survives. An even earlier house, on the same site, dated back to the time of the Crusades. Birch Hall was another black and white building, probably dating back to the 16th century, and demolished in 1926 to make way for Manchester Grammar School, built in 1931.

Agriculture would be the principal occupation for the people in the 16th to 18th centuries, but during the 17th and 18th centuries, cottage industries began to flourish. The agricultural population of earlier centuries had probably been self-sufficient in most respects, but now more and more workers began to specialise, and to make a

3

Within the image, handwritten: *exactly* *Rusholme* *"opposite*

Victoria Park Gates, Oxford Place, c.1904

The pedimented and columned front of the lodge is typical of the classical front of many, if not all, of Richard Lane's public buildings, e.g. Friends' Meeting House, Mount Street, Manchester, the former Chorlton-on-Medlock Town Hall, All Saints, and Stockport Infirmary.

The roads were privately maintained by the Park residents until 1957 when the Corporation remade them to bye-law standards (and at the frontagers' expense) over a period of some five years.

Manchester Grammar School, Old Hall Lane, 1939

At the outbreak of war in 1939, feverish efforts were made to prepare for the expected air raids. These protective measures paid off in 1941, when a large bomb fell in front of the school, damaging houses on Old Hall Lane, but leaving unscathed the sand-bagged ground floor of the school.

living wholly from occupations unrelated to agriculture, e.g. spinning, weaving, brickmaking, shoemaking, ropemaking, roadmaking, and – the beginnings of bureaucracy – Poor Law administration. The American Civil War brought starvation to the cotton weavers of South East Lancashire, and it is from this period that the first eye witness accounts of facets of life in Rusholme date. William Royle of Rusholme, and Mrs. Williamson of Fallowfield were the principal recorders of local events in this area during the 19th century. The statue of Abraham Lincoln in front of Platt Hall is a reminder "of Lancashire's friendship to the cause for which he lived and died", and of the near-starvation to which the cotton workers were reduced by the cotton famine which followed the blockading of the ports of the Southern States.

The 19th century in Rusholme was largely the story of gradual change from an agricultural/cottage-industry economy to a suburban residential area. From 1830 to 1870, many large mansions were built in Victoria Park and along Wilmslow Road, with even more houses for the working classes going up in the old Rusholme village area centred on Nelson Street, between Platt Lane and Claremont Road. But from 1870 onwards there was a tremendous increase in building, during which every available site was used for small and medium-sized houses. These changes were brought about by the increased demand for labour in the Manchester factories and warehouses, by the movement of population from central Manchester – first by the merchants, then by the professional classes, and finally by the workers – and by the influx of population from the surrounding countryside and from further afield. Germany, Scotland, Wales, and, in particular, Ireland were the source of much of this movement.

But immigration on this scale could not have occurred without improvements in communications; Wilmslow Road was turnpiked in the

1770's, the railways came in mid 19th century, horse trams were running as far as Fallowfield by 1880, and granite sett road surfaces were laid shortly afterwards.

By the end of the century, development of the area was practically complete, and a period of comparative stability followed, though it was not to last. Development of the internal combustion engine completely changed the aspect of our streets from one of slow moving horsedrawn traffic and electric tramcars, to that which we know today – high volumes of car, bus, and lorry traffic, with their accompanying pollution, noise, (and convenience).

The most notable phenomenon of the 1960's and 1970's was the new wave of immigration, which, once again, could hardly have occurred without the remarkable improvements in travel opportunities presented by the jet airliner. West Indian and – in particular – Asian families arrived in substantial numbers in those years, and their shopkeepers have transformed the character of retail shopping in Rusholme.

Finally, it would be impossible to exclude from a review of the history of Rusholme the impact made by the post-war expansion of Manchester University. Halls of Residence have sprung up, or have been expanded, in Victoria Park and along Wilmslow Road; and University students, unable to find a place in Hall, have become lodgers in, or tenants of, many houses in the area.

Fallowfield

The pattern of Fallowfield's growth is similar to that of Rusholme's. Early records describe it as an open area with a few farming settlements. The origin of the name Fallowfield also describes its early character; it means literally, "fallow field". In his book *The place names of Lancashire,* Ekwall explains that this would have meant an uncultivated area rather than cultivated land being allowed to lie fallow or unused for a period. He traces various spellings which have appeared:

Fallafeld in 1317, Falofield in 1417, and Falowfelde in 1530. In the 1300's, the land was held by Jordan de Fallowfield and his family; it was the practice of those times for important families to assume the name of their area as their surname.

Over the centuries there was little change; readers of Mrs. Linnaeus Banks' novel *The Manchester Man,* will remember that her heroine Augusta lived in an elegant mansion in Fallowfield during her marriage to the dashing but dastardly Lawrence Aspinall. This would have been around the 1820's, when Fallowfield is described as being "remote from town, and sparsely populated". Johnson's map on page 7 shows just a few large houses – Ashfield, The Oaks, The Firs, Mabfield, and Cabbage Hall – set in open fields.

Mrs. Williamson in her book *Sketches of Fallowfield,* draws a charming picture of Fallowfield in the early nineteenth century before the effects of the industrial revolution – it was a green and peaceful area of pretty farms, winding lanes, trout streams, and fields of golden corn. Her descriptions of the scenery may be a bit flowery, but a gentle sarcasm enters her tales of village entertainments. During the Fallowfield Wakes, the rush cart – which "consisted of a wonderful erection of rushes built upon a farmer's flat cart, decorated with garlands, branches of oak, ribbons, flags, tinsel, everything that ingenuity and bad taste could devise, and often completed by a Robin Hood and Maid Marian, who, more grotesque than all else, were seated on top of the rushes" – was paraded around the district. Apparently the noise was tremendous; "pipers played the well-known Rush Dance; clogs which then everyone wore, beat time; children's penny whistles accompanied; and the shouts of all the people drowned, or tried to do so, this medley of sound". Not all residents were satisfied with music, dancing, and parades; others got their enjoyment from bull and bear-baiting.

However, with the industrial boom of the

nineteenth century, Manchester's population started to move out of the city centre to places like Fallowfield. Mrs. Williamson noted the change by the 1850's – "old landed proprietors showed themselves willing to sell, the younger men willing to speculate; this was the beginning of the end of Old Fallowfield". Norton House and Norton Villas, Egerton Lodge and Oak House were built; in 1861 Alfred Waterhouse, architect of Manchester Town Hall, designed Barcombe Cottage on Oak Drive as his own residence. More houses, roads, schools, and shops were completed, and the farms gave way to the twentieth century.

Improvements in transport – Fallowfield railway station opened in 1891, and a tram service along Wilbraham Road connecting Chorlton and Fallowfield opened in 1924 – facilitated this flight

Wilmslow Road at Platt Bridge, c.1910

Increased traffic, generated by the upsurge of house building in the suburbs in the preceding 20 years, made the widening of roads a necessity. Here is Wilmslow Road, almost opposite Norman Road, Platt Estate wall has been taken down and set back to form the boundary wall of the "new" park (Platt Fields), thus allowing the road to be widened. On the left, partly obscured by the lamp standard, are the two entrance columns of Brighton Grove, and, beyond them, the lodge of the large house called Appleby Lodge. This lodge was one of a pair built for the projected Brighton Grove Scheme, of large houses to be built round a lake. It was made use of as the lodge of Appleby Lodge, when that house was built on land which was to have been the lake and southern part of the Scheme.

to the green suburbs. Fallowfield was absorbed into Manchester, the Rusholme section in 1885 and the Withington section in 1904. The burden of providing services such as transport, water, and sewerage became the task of the city, although districts such as Fallowfield, Rusholme and Withington, were often loth to give up their independence.

Today it is a residential area with a large student population. Little industry developed over the years; the nineteenth century arrivals were fleeing the mills, and would not have wanted them built in their pretty new neighbourhood, and the shopping centre did not grow to the same size as those of its neighbours Rusholme and Withington. However, the large houses which we can still see along Wilmslow Road and Wilbraham Road, rival the mansions of Victoria Park, and show that parts of Fallowfield were once rather grand.

The boundaries of Fallowfield have always been a little hard to define, it seems often to be a sort of left-over area, dominated by the larger villages of Rusholme and Withington, and it wasn't until

1982 that it elected its own councillors.

As an ecclesiastical parish however, it was more clearly defined. With the completion of Holy Innocents Church, the new parish was created in 1873, drawn partly from Rusholme and partly from Withington. Mrs. Williamson described the area: "The district assigned to the new Parish is on the Didsbury, now Wilmslow Road. It is bounded north by Platt Brook, or Old Hall Lane; south by Ley Brook or Brook Road; its eastern boundary is Shooting Gallery or Whitworth's Lane; an extension runs along Mauldeth Road in the direction of Burnage; westward the parish extends a considerable distance along Wilbraham Road; from which it sends out a tongue northward along Dog Kennel Path; this western portion includes Demesne Farm, Dog House and Old Hall Farms, and reaches to within a stone's throw of Hough End Hall".

This has been a brief look at the histories of Rusholme and Fallowfield. The following map and photographs will illustrate aspects of their growth and character.

Part of Johnson's map of Manchester of 1838 *right*

The Rusholme boundary in 1838 is shown by a shaded grey line. Most of what we now consider to be Fallowfield was then in Withington, an arm of which extended northwards as far as Clock House Lane (Moss Lane East). There has never been an administrative area of Fallowfield, and only recently an electoral ward. The boundary of Rusholme runs off the right-hand edge of the map to include farmland on the borders of Burnage. Wilmslow Road is the road which runs from the northern (top) edge of the map, and out at the southern (bottom) edge passing through Rusholme in the centre of the map. Named streets which have been subsequently renamed are Clock House Lane (now Moss Lane East), Ladybarn Lane (now Mauldeth Road), and Old Hall Lane (now Old Moat Lane). Dog Kennel Lane (now Maine Road) is the lane shown between Clock House Lane and Dog Kennel. Demesne Farm was near the corner of Platt Lane and Yew Tree Road. Rusholme House was on what is now Whitworth Park. This house was once the home of Major General Sir Harry Smith and Lady Smith (after whom Ladysmith and Harrismith in South Africa were named). William Royle remembers "his erect military figure as he used to ride about the village, his breast covered with medals, on his famous charger, Aliwal". On its death, the horse was buried in the garden of Rusholme House near a stone engraved with the horse's history. Sadly, the stone has disappeared, probably being destroyed when the house was demolished.

Tollgate at the corner of Mauldeth Road and Wilmslow Road, c.189

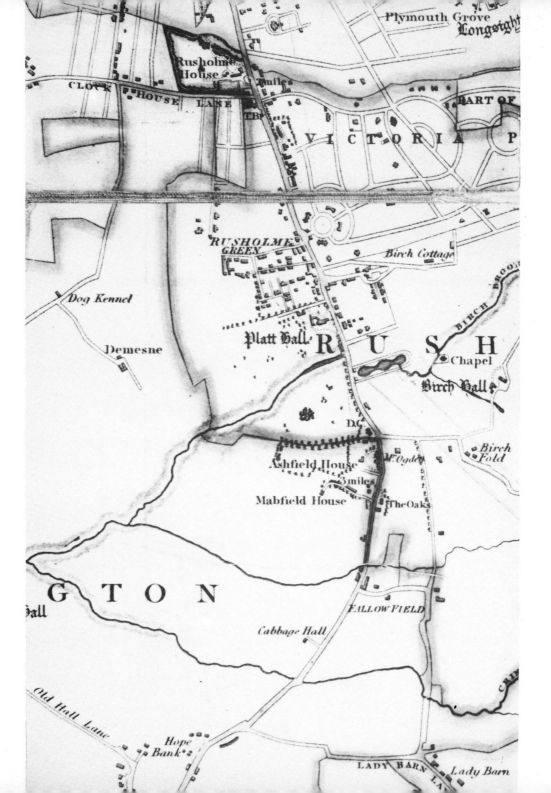

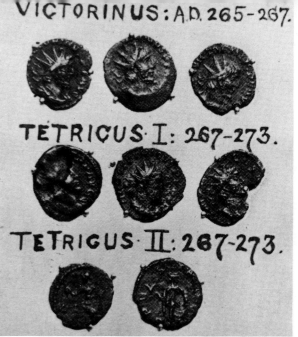

VICTORINUS: A.D. 265-267.

TETRICUS I: 267-273.

TETRICUS II: 267-273.

The Roman coins found near Gore Brook.

On Wilmslow Road, just south of the junction with Clock House Lane (Moss Lane East), can be seen the letters T B. This was the Toll Bar which stood approximately where Harrod's Depository is now. It was put there in the 18th century to levy tolls for construction and repair of Wilmslow Road.

Map makers at this period tended to anticipate proposed developments, and they were sometimes caught out when the proposals came to nothing. On this map there are examples at the east end of Victoria Park (near the right-hand border), and the link road from Rusholme Grove to Birch Cottage; and, most notable of all, the proposed development of mansions and landscaped lake at Brighton Grove (below the "U" of RUSH(OLME) on this map). Only the building occupied by the Liverpool Victoria Friendly Society, facing Wilmslow Road, survives from that scheme. South of this site can be seen the letters D C, which represent Dissenting Chapel, i.e. Platt Chapel, now the home of Manchester Amateur Photographic Society. Of the group of houses south of Platt Chapel only "Mr. Ogden's" house still stands. It is now the nucleus of Ashburne Hall (a University Hall of Residence). Of Fallowfield itself only a tiny group of houses, near the corner of Ladybarn Road and Wilmslow Road, are represented, the remaining buildings being farm houses.

7

Ladies requiring ::
GOOD SERVANTS
— AND —
Servants Reliable ::
SITUATIONS

PLEASE CALL OR WRITE

MRS. DUTTON,

VICTORIA PARK REGISTRY,

39 Dickenson Rd., Rusholme.

OFFICE HOURS: 10 to 1, and 2 to 5 o'clock.

MAIDS until 8 o'clock.   SATURDAYS 10 to 1 only.

Advertisement for Servants, 1913 *above*

This advertisement which appeared in the South
Manchester Almanack for 1913, gives a good
indication of the social order in Victoria Park before the
First World War.

Ordnance Survey Map, 1890's *left*

The map of Rusholme and Fallowfield in the 1890's
shows that this part of Manchester – both Rusholme
and Withington had by then been incorporated into the
City – was still rural. Some areas of small houses had
been built in Rusholme, but Fallowfield's farms were
still active, and housing was restricted to quite a narrow
area on either side of Wilmslow Road, most of the
houses being large and detached. The railway has
arrived, and has a substantial area of sidings at
Fallowfield Station. Moseley Road has not yet been
built, and Wilbraham Road is still a privately gated
road.

Victoria Park – an elegant anachronism

Victoria Park started as a splendidly Victorian scheme to provide building plots on which palatial houses could be built for important people. A company was set up to purchase land in the Rusholme area, the land being then sold in blocks to shareholders and speculators. Richard Lane, the architect, was given the task of planning the layout of the Park. He based it on three crescents, Park Crescent, Hanover Crescent, and a third crescent – crossing Laindon Road – which was never built. Each house was to have large gardens; many trees were planted, and toll gates were placed round the boundaries, so that outsiders would have to pay if they wished to ride or drive through such a select neighbourhood. The Park opened in 1837, and in that year an Act of Parliament was passed to consolidate the position of the Company.

However, in 1839 the Company failed, and for a while Lane's dream went awry. The landowners held a meeting in 1845, when it was decided that a Victoria Park Trust would be formed to carry out the original concept, and a committee was elected to manage the Park's affairs.

For many years all went smoothly. Splendid houses continued to be built for Manchester's wealthy merchants; artists, activists and reformers also settled in the Park. Ford Madox Brown, Charles Halle, and Mrs. Pankhurst lived in houses on Daisy Bank Road. Leading parliamentarians such as George Hadfield, Richard Cobden, and Sir Henry Roscoe were residents.

It couldn't last. Running costs for those large houses must have been enormous, and after the First World War, servants would no longer work for a pittance. Improved transport meant that people could move further out of Manchester. Terraces and semis were being built, and the area was no longer as select as it had been. The building of the Anson estate on the old Anson Golf Club land was probably the final blow. The increase in traffic along Anson Road led to considerable public pressure to remove the tolls, and in 1938 the road was thrown open. The Trust then installed toll gates on the side roads, but it was a last ditch effort, and the last toll gate was removed in 1954. Many of the large houses became institutions of one sort or another; university halls of residence, schools and nursing homes.

Today the Park has an assured future. Part of the original Park was declared a Conservation Area in 1976. This means that no building may be demolished, or altered in any way that adversely affects its architectural character, without the agreement of the City Council. Victoria Park can never be what it was, but some of its architectural glories will remain.

Richard Lane's House, Oxford Place, 1930's

The Park's designer, Richard Lane, lived for a short time in one of the elegant mansions situated in the estate which he created. Victoria Park opened with much ceremony on July 31st 1837. A procession of thirteen carriages filled with Manchester dignitaries entered the Park, and were welcomed by a band playing the National Anthem. They then proceeded to Mr. Lane's house, where the proud owner showed them over his grounds and offered them refreshments. It must have been a great day for Richard Lane.

Park Crescent entrance to Victoria Park, *below*

Two views of the same entrance to Victoria Park, but separated in time by 73 years. The 1866 view is a very early photograph, and it shows the toll gate on Wilmslow Road before it was moved back towards the Crescent, when the present shops on Wilmslow Road were built. Note the lodges on either side of the entrance. These were designed by Richard Lane and show his enthusiasm for the classical style of architecture. The toll house in the 1939 photograph is a much more humble hut, a good illustration of how Victoria Park had retreated.

Park Crescent entrance to Victoria Park, 1939

By this time Wilmslow Road was a busy thoroughfare lined with shops, hardly a suitable spot to stop traffic to collect tolls before it entered the Park.

The land in the middle of the Crescent is fenced off with iron railings. Certain residents used to have the right to a pie wedge of this land, but it was declared common ground by the Park Committee sometime between the wars, after unneighbourly quarrels arose between some owners who wanted to build upon their sections.

Anson Road, with Upper Brook Street beyond the toll gate c.1925 *right*

The toll gate and the tram lines in this picture are both symbols of the struggle of the Park to remain unmoved by the Corporation's plans to change with the times. Anson Road within Victoria Park did not have trams until 1920, although the Corporation had attempted as long ago as 1902 to negotiate an agreement to lay track through the Park. The hut was eventually removed some years after the Corporation built the Anson Estate. In the Chief Constable's report for 1938, this road was the second busiest road out of Manchester, only Stockport Road exceeding it in density of traffic. Obviously the removal of the toll gates in 1938 had made a difference to the traffic volume!

Corner of Upper Park Road and Denison Road, Victoria Park before 1970 *below right*

This pair of Italianate houses were at the corner of Upper Park Road and Denison Road, on a site now occupied by the Regent House flats. E. R. Langworthy – one time Mayor of Salford – who lived in the building which is now Langdale Hall, on the opposite corner of Upper Park Road, also owned the land on which these, and two more identical houses were built in 1853, to the design of Manchester architect Edward Walters. On this picture, they are, from right to left, South Villa, Ivy Villa, and a corner of Elbe Villa. At some date after 1911, the widow of Louis Grommé, who had lived in Regent House (now Marylands, Lower Park Road) since 1888, moved into South Villa. The story goes that she was so attached to the name that she renamed South Villa as Regent House, which name is now carried by the flats on the site. The house on the extreme left (Elbe Villa) was occupied by a Mr. Hilditch in the 1920's. He had amassed a large collection of Oriental Wares about which there was much controversy, many experts maintaining that the collection was mostly of fakes. At his death, the collection was dispersed, but some pieces from it have recently been traced and found to be genuine. Shortly before the demolition (about 1970), the house was converted to a mosque, and, soon afterwards, on the site of Elbe Villa and West View (the other half of the semi) the present mosque buildings were erected.

Church of St. John Chrysostom, Anson Road, 1904 *above*

The church of St. John Chrysostom on Anson Road was built between 1874 and 1876 at a cost of £13,000, and was consecrated by Bishop Fraser on the 13th October, 1877. The congregation would have been quite mixed; this new parish included both the wealthy families of the Park and their servants, and the areas of poor housing in Chorlton-on-Medlock.

Things went smoothly for the new church until 1904, when it was gutted by fire. The warden at Ashburne Hall, then opposite the church, described the fire as "one of those sights which leave an impression for the rest of one's life. The whole of the roof of the church was in flames, and no-one who has not seen such a thing, can imagine the volume of fire that coiled up with a ceaseless roar, the great clouds of thick smoke, the sparks falling in showers, slate after slate crashing down from the roof, glass cracking and splintering as the fire shot through window after window".*

Unfortunately, the water supply was not functioning properly. The building was only insured for £8,950, as no-one had thought it possible that the church could be almost totally destroyed. The Committee for rebuilding, noted a further problem in a pamphlet appealing for funds. "The neighbourhood has very much changed during the past 27 years, and whilst the resident churchmen have largely contributed according to their ability, the number of those from whom substantial aid can be expected, is considerably reduced." Twentieth century winds of change had started to blow over Victorian Victoria Park.

However, fund-raising was eventually successful, and the church was rebuilt and re-opened in 1906. Whilst the work was going on, the parishioners had to make do with a temporary iron church on Anson Road, at the corner of Daisy Bank Road, which was demolished when the church was re-opened.

Extract from Yggdrasil (The Ashburne Chronicle) for 1904.

Ashburne House, corner of Conyngham Road and Oxford Place, Victoria Park, c.1900 *below*

Ashburne House was built in 1849. Over the years it had a typically Victoria Park succession of residents – public figures, politicians, merchants and students. Robert Barbour was the first owner; he was associated with the re-foundation of Manchester Grammar School. William Romaine Callender (jnr.) was the next owner. He entertained Disraeli at Ashburne House during one of his visits to Manchester, and thus outraged his father William Romaine Callender (snr.) at Hopeville (later Brookfield Hotel) in Oxford Place, who strongly disapproved of Disraeli and his politics. The merchants followed – Harry M. Lazerus, and then Bernard Alexander. This period of private ownership ceased, and the students moved in. In the early years of the century, Ashburne House became Ashburne Hall, one of the university's halls of residence. When Ashburne Hall moved to its present site at the corner of Old Hall Lane and Wilmslow Road, the former Ashburne House was renamed Egerton Hall, and became a Theological College.

During its last ten years, Ashburne was let as flats, and allowed to run down. It was demolished about 1970, a fate from which – thanks to the current emphasis on preserving the Victorian splendours of the Park – similar buildings have been spared. The site has been redeveloped as Ashburne House flats.

Ashburne House, Victoria Park

RUSHOLME THEATRE

Manager: Mr. HARRY LISTON (of "Merry Moments" fame).

High-class Cinematograph

Change of Pictures every Monday and Thursday.

ADMISSION:

3d. :: **6d.** :: **9d.**

plus 1d Tax, 4d	plus 1d Tax, 7d	plus 2d Tax, 11d
Early Doors, Saturday Nights and Holidays, 4d	Early Doors, Saturday Nights 9d	Early Doors, Saturday Nights and Holidays, 1/2
plus 1d Tax, 5d	plus 2d Tax, 11d	
Half-price 1½d plus ½d Tax, 2d	Half-price 3d	plus 2d Tax, 1/2

IMPORTANT NOTICE.

No Seats guaranteed after 6·50 and 9 o'clock.

The Management reserve the right to refuse admission.

The Company will not be responsible for payment of any goods delivered, without signed order from the Manager.

The Tram Depot

Wilmslow Road near Great Western Street, c.1904

This end of Wilmslow Road has seen some changes, although the row of shops is much the same today, and Harrod's Depository on the left, built in 1876, is still with us. The photograph was taken before the widening of Wilmslow Road to cope with the trams and the increase in traffic; the new kerb line is just to the left of the foreground tram standard.

The building on the left, about level with the tram, has had a varied history. It was originally the depot for the Manchester Carriage and Tramways Company's horses and horse trams. When the Company ceased to run horse trams in 1901, the depot was taken over by a riding school. In 1910 the premises were re-opened as the Rusholme Electric Theatre, which ran programmes of films and variety turns. In 1923, Mr. Belt formed the Rusholme Repertory Theatre, and used the buildings to run hundreds of shows, including Walter Greenwood's Love on the Dole, and also The Prisoner of Zenda, Pygmalion, Wuthering Heights and She Stoops to Conquer. However, the premises were never really suitable, and the company had almost continual financial difficulties. Although it had given enjoyment to thousands of people, its days of live theatre were over, and the building was converted to a cinema about 1940. This cinema closed about 1970, but opened again to show Asian films, until fire damage resulted in its complete closure in 1982.

Wilmslow Road, Rusholme

Congregational Church, Wilmslow Road, early 1970's *below left*

A rather depressing photograph of the Rusholme Congregational Church on Wilmslow Road, some time before its demolition in 1978. It hardly looks the sort of place for the wedding of a future Prime Minister, although this did happen in 1877 when Herbert H. Asquith, a rising young barrister, married Miss Helen Melland.

The Congregational Church was first established in Rusholme in 1839 as a Sunday School, then later as a chapel in Kingthorpe Grove at the bottom of Moor Street. A new chapel opened in Moor Street in 1853. The church in this photograph was opened in 1864.

The total cost was £7,000 and there were 650 sittings. The clock in the tower was illuminated, and many Rusholme people, in the days before most people had watches, must have glanced at that clock during the day and night for the time.

Wilmslow Road, near the corner of Walmer Street, c.1905 *below right*

The electric tram transformed the Rusholme street. Only four years earlier, everything had been horse-drawn, but by 1905, there were 550 electric trams on the road, operating a frequent service. The single deck car was operating what is now the 53 route. All the buildings on the left were demolished during the redevelopment of the Walmer Street area, but the shops on the right can still be seen.

The Rusholme Local Board of Health buildings, corner of Claremont Road and Heald Place, mid 1960's *above left*

The Rusholme Local Board of Health was formed in 1849 to organise the public health services in the area. This is how Royle writes of its beginnings. "The meetings to arrange its establishment were held in Dr. Melland's house in Wilmslow Road, at the corner with Moor Street. They were attended by Mr. T. Lowe, Mr. E. R. Langworthy, Rev. G. H. G. Anson, Dr. Melland and one or two others. All honour to these men, the pioneers of public work in Rusholme. Prior to this time, many of the streets of the village were undrained and unpaved, and the sides of them were almost open sewers. Monmouth Street (now Claremont Road) and Walmer Street were then, in wet weather, ankle-deep in mud, but the Board effected many improvements. It was in 1853 that for the first time, Corporation water was introduced. Streets were paved and sewered, and the foundations were then laid for the excellent system of drainage which we now enjoy, and I venture to affirm that Rusholme is one of the healthiest spots in Manchester." This passage is so typical of Royle, showing as it does, his great affection and enthusiasm for Rusholme and his willingness to praise those who worked for its improvement – probably none worked as hard as Royle himself.

Built in the last years of Rusholme's independence before it was absorbed into Manchester, the offices in this photograph would appear to indicate a confidence that Rusholme would continue to govern its afairs for some time to come. This didn't happen, but at one time the local health, fire, mortuary and abattoir services, were all in this small area of Rusholme. The building was finally demolished in 1983.

REAL ICE SKATING RINK AT RUSHOLME, NOW OPEN

Skating at the Ice Skating Rink, Moor Street, c.1877 *above right*

This contemporary drawing of the proceedings inside the rink, show Rusholmites completely at ease as they skate to the music of an orchestra.

Moor Street, from Wilmslow Road, c.1905 *below*

On the corner at the left is the Rusholme Coffee Tavern; then, on the left-hand side in Moor Street, the whitewashed blacksmith's shop of John Whittaker. At the right-hand edge of the picture is the house which, until 1871, had been the home of Dr. Melland, whose daughter Helen was the first wife of Mr. H. H. Asquith, later to become Prime Minister. Beyond this house, and between the two wall-mounted gas lamps which can be seen on the right, is the Rusholme Real Ice Skating Rink, reputed to have been the first ice rink in England, but already closed by this time (1905).

In the foreground of this photograph are three boys, the centre one wearing knickerbockers and boots, the one on the right in the uniform of the Corporation's Transport Department. He was almost certainly the "point-boy" from the corner of Dickenson Road and Wilmslow Road. It was his job to operate the points so that trams on the 53 route turned left along Dickenson Road, and all others continued along Wilmslow Road.

The Primitive Methodist Church, Moor Street, Rusholme, c.1938 *left*

In addition to the Wesleyan Chapel in Dickenson Road, Methodism had another location in Rusholme. This photograph shows the Primitive Methodist Church on Moor Street. It was built during the 1840's. When this photograph was taken, around 1938, the building was no longer used as a church, and had been divided into two dwellings with a rather rickety front porch tacked on. The stone with the original name can be seen over the front doors.

Claremont Road, opposite Fleeson Street, c.1965 *below left*

These houses were contemporary with those in the Nelson Street area behind them, and were demolished with the rest of old Rusholme village about 1970. They stood between the Police Station, which would be the next building on the left after the entry, and the Lord Lyon public house, the cement-rendered gable of which is at the right of the picture. Only the Lord Lyon, of that group, survives.

Corner of Moor Street and Wilmslow Road, c.1950 *below right*

The Temperance Bar was once the coffee shop where the early Rusholme library was housed, and where the Rusholme worthies of the Victorian era would have met for books, conversation and coffee. On the right is the Trocadero cinema still open in 1950, but now closed, like so many other suburban cinemas. The Congregational Church looms over the roofs of the shops. The Kwik Save supermarket occupies part of the site of the Trocadero, and council houses have replaced the nineteenth century buildings.

The traction pole, or tram standard as it was colloquially known, was a relic of the tram service along Wilmslow Road. Buses replaced the trams in 1938, but the section from Dickenson Road to Moss Lane East, was retained until 1945 for some workmen's services. After that, the poles remained for many years, until they were replaced by purpose-built street lighting poles.

Summer Place, early 1970's *above left*

Summer Place is of the same era and style as Nelson Place, and was demolished at the same time. Neville Cardus was born at No. 2 Summer Place, in 1891. He was an extraordinary man; there is probably no-one else in the history of journalism who has been both a music critic and a cricket commentator. When he died in 1975, he was a much-loved national figure. In his autobiography, he has described this area as a slum, although some would disagree with this description.

Cardus wrote of his childhood in Rusholme with a mixture of irony and affection. His first experience of cricket was on a pitch at the local Corporation tip . . "During the summer, cricket was played on these open spaces. Given a library and a cricket pitch, both free-of-charge, I was obviously blessed with good luck beyond the lot of most boys, rich or poor. Here at any rate was the material I needed".

He attended the local board school, which he saw as a place of "darkness and inhumanity", and his family took in washing for the local better-offs. Young Neville, when he wasn't at school reading or playing cricket, used to help in the family business by delivering rush orders in an old perambulator.

Junction of Wilmslow Road and Dickenson Road, c.1965 *above right*

The Casino Cinema closed around 1962 after it was damaged by fire, and the Rusholme Congregational Church seen on the right has gone. Some things remain however. Rusholme Gardens, which opened as a rather refined block of flats in 1923, is still there. The Chas. Wilson garage has moved a little further down the road, but business goes on, and the Invisible Mending sign hasn't altered. After Roy Clarke finished his playing career with Manchester City, he opened the sports shop seen on the left of the picture. After a few years, he moved to larger premises on the corner of Dickenson Road, but this larger shop subsequently became a betting shop, and Rusholme no longer has a sports shop.

Nelson Place, off Platt Lane, early 1970's *right*

These houses show the architectural style of the older cottages which formed the village of Rusholme before the building boom of the later years of the 1800's. All of the houses in this area were demolished during the 1970's to make way for council housing, despite the fact that many were in good condition. Rusholme was almost the last of the areas in which wholesale clearance of large areas was carried out, with the result that former residents could no longer recognise their old surroundings.

Dickenson Road, Wilmslow Road corner, c.1920 *left*

Birch Villa Hotel is easily recognisable, but there are many things in this photograph that have since disappeared – Leslie's Pavilion which can just be seen on the right for example, the Congregational Church and the buildings immediately beyond it, the cobbles and the tram lines . . . The road looks almost empty when you consider the traffic that rushes along there today.

Leslie's Pavilion, Wilmslow Road, 1934 *below left*

With the Rusholme Repertory Theatre and Leslie's Pavilion, Rusholme was well provided with live theatre. Leslie's Pavilion opened in 1905 and closed 34 years later, when the war made it almost impossible to find artists. Over the years it featured many shows, particularly variety and comedy such as "Leslie's Comedy Cadets" and "Middies and Maids". Music was also offered, with choir evenings and what the programme referred to as "high class promenade concerts".

This photograph is an interesting one – drag queens in Rusholme, presented by Miss Billie Manders. One wonders what the Cotton Queen (Alice Kirkham) thought about it. The Cotton Queen herself was promoted by the now defunct "Daily Dispatch"; each year the winner was an honoured guest at festivals and celebrations, a figurehead of the industry which made Manchester a household name. In all parts of the Empire, department stores had a section known as the "Manchester Department" which sold cotton goods from the mills of Lancashire. Nowadays there are no Cotton Queens, nor is there much of a cotton industry.

Harry Leslie is the formally-dressed man on the Cotton Queen's right. Until he was 28, Harry Makinson worked as a clerk in a Manchester yarn office, but by that age he had tired of the office, and left to pursue his theatrical ambitions as Harry Leslie. He worked as a comic and ventriloquist at various seaside resorts, and later established his own theatre, first in a tent and later, on the same site, his own theatre – Leslie's Pavilion.

Rusholme Library, Dickenson Road, c.1960 *right*

This photograph shows Rusholme Public Hall and Library around the 1960's. The library was originally housed in a building known as the Coffee Tavern, on the corner of Wilmslow Road and Moor Street. A public meeting of Rusholme people decided that their library needed better premises, so land was purchased on Dickenson Road, and the Rusholme Public Hall and Reading Room was built on the site, and was opened in January, 1860. The total cost of £3,000, was raised by public subscription. Two bazaars brought in some money, whilst Rusholme notables such as C. Carill-Worsley, E. R. Langworthy, Sir William Anson, W. Entwistle, Robert Barnes, Robert Barbour, Ivie Mackie, Samuel Royle and W. R. Callender, made substantial donations. Mackie was Mayor of Manchester in 1860, and Barnes a former Mayor.

After the Rusholme Local Board area was absorbed into Manchester in 1885, the library was administered by its trustees for a period, but in 1891 it was transferred to the Corporation to continue as a free library and reading room for the general public. The building was demolished about 1970.

"Manchester A.R.P. Control Centre No. 6", 1940 *left*

This is the scene inside the basement of Rusholme Library & Public Hall – opposite the Birch Villa car park – in the early days of the war. The control centre presumably received reports of "incidents" from the A.R.P. (Air Raid Precautions) Wardens on the streets, and organised the movement of police, fire tenders and ambulances, as circumstances required. All communication would be by telephone (or on foot or bicycle, if the telephone service was affected by enemy action). Notice the two pillar-type telephones in front of the police constable at the left of the picture, the steel joists and pillars supporting the ceiling, the kitchen chairs, and the lamp bulbs with pre-war glass shades.

19

The original chapel

Dickenson Road

Ladybarn Lane

Dickenson Road Methodist Church, early 1970's

This church started its life as the Wesleyan Church, Rusholme, and finished as a television studio for the B.B.C. A memorial window, dedicated to the memory of William Royle, was unveiled there in 1924.

Methodism was started in Rusholme by Charles Beswick, a preacher from Ardwick, who opened the first Sunday School in Rusholme in 1826 in Claremont Road. In 1829, a chapel was built on Dickenson Road. It was taken down brick by brick in 1863, and re-erected with two storeys added, as a working men's club in Ladybarn Lane. The two photographs show the transformation. The new church was opened in 1862, and closed as a church about 1940.

During the 1940's and 1950's, this building housed a film studio which turned out a succession of money spinning comedy films, and earned Rusholme the title of Manchester's Hollywood.

On the left of the 1862 Church can be seen the end of the building known as "Little Birch" – the infants department of (St. James) Birch Schools. On the right of the same picture is part of the gable end, with an oriel window, of the Post Office Engineering workshop. It was originally a telephone exchange, until superseded by the newer building next door, and was demolished in 1982 to allow a third extension to be built onto the present exchange. (The first Rusholme telephone exchange was in a house in Rusholme Grove (No. 2), now demolished.)

Dickenson Road/Conyngham Road corner, 1914 *left*

Another example of a road before widening; this section of Dickenson Road was widened on the right-hand side, so that those front garden trees are now on the pavement. The piece of land advertised for sale, together with the site of the large terraced houses in the centre of the photograph, is now occupied by an estate of houses built between 1958 and 1962. Note the decorative cast iron sleeves at the base of the tram standards; these were removed all over Manchester, and, together with iron railings and other scrap, were used in the war effort. The tram standards themselves were not replaced until 1984, having been used for street lighting purposes for the last 40 years of their life.

Birch Park Skating Palace, Anson Road, early 1960's *inset*

Remember the roller-skating rink and Brian Poole and the Tremoloes? Those whose memories don't include the 1960's, will know the building as Oceans 11, or as Genevieve's night club, or, more recently, The Sting.

The low-level buildings to the left of Hanson's shop, which look rather like allotment huts, were actually pre-fab council houses, built as a temporary measure to alleviate the post-war housing shortage.

Birchfields Road from Dickenson Road, *right*

This is an interesting photograph in that it shows how open and empty this part of Rusholme was, around the turn of the century. On the right is Birchfields Park, opened in 1888. The trees in the park are still saplings, with the now-demolished bandstand showing over them. Rusholme was still rural – the man in the field on the left is on horseback, and a farm barn can be seen in the distance, near where Meldon Road is now. The road has been built only as far as Birch Hall Lane, and is narrower where the Gore Brook flows beneath it. The group of houses beyond the brook, are on the corner of Birchfields Avenue.

The Culverting of Gore Brook, early 1920's

Before work on the Anson Estate could commence, Gore Brook had to be culverted and covered. "Gore" is an old English word for dirty, and some people feel this describes Gore Brook very nicely, and that to cover its entire length would be the decent thing to do. However, it can look pretty as it flows through Birchfields Park and around Birch Church, so perhaps it's best kept as it is. The building with the verandah, on the left of this picture, is the clubhouse for the golf course which once occupied the area of today's Anson Estate. The houses on the left are in Sunny Bank Road (off Dickenson Road), and the factory-like building behind the crane bucket, was the Co-operative Printing Works at the corner of Hamilton Road and Stamford Road, Longsight. The section to the right of the bucket was demolished about 1970.

The internal combustion engine was still in its infancy, and all heavy plant – such as this crane – would be steam-powered, and would use temporary railway track.

Birchfields Park, Rusholme, c.1913 *below*

A day in the park for most of Rusholme. Note the boaters and the bandstand. Birchfields park was opened by Prince Albert Victor in October 1888. Its genesis was a mixture of politicking and benevolence. When Rusholme was absorbed into Manchester in 1885, the Rusholme Local Board made incorporation conditional on the city purchasing Birchfields Park for public use. Mr. Herbert Phillips added 4½ acres of land which he owned on Dickenson Road, and Sir William Anson gave 5 acres.

Reporting the official opening of the Park, the Manchester Guardian on 22nd October 1888, had this to say:– "At the entrance to the new recreation grounds, there was a great crowd of spectators, and the Prince was received with a good deal of enthusiasm. In front of the gates he was presented with a gold key by Mr. Chesters Thompson, Chairman of the Parks Committee . . . The Prince accepted the key, and shook hands with the Parks Committee, presented by the Mayor. H.R.H. then unlocked the gates, and passing through a crimson arch, ascended a platform and declared the grounds open. The band should have come in at this point with the National Anthem. It did not, and the silence which followed the cheering, was broken by the strong voice of the Chairman of the Parks Committee, uplifted in song. The spectators joined in, and the National Anthem was given with great effect . . ".

Barrage Balloon, Birchfields Park, c.1940 *inset*

At the outbreak of the 1939–1945 war, Manchester residents were surprised to see that dozens of barrage balloons had been deployed in parks and open spaces throughout the city, in an attempt to protect the population from the effects of dive bombing and low-flying bombers, which had been such a feature of the Spanish Civil War. Very often the balloons were moored at ground level as in this picture, but when all were high in the sky, they produced a wonderful visual effect in addition to the feeling of reassurance felt by the people below them. This balloon site is in Birchfields Park, close to the Gore Brook, and to the one-time bandstand.

Birch Chapel, c.1800 *right*

It would be impossible to write about the history of Rusholme without mentioning the name of Birch. The family, the ancient Chapel, and later the Church, have played an important part in the village's life for centuries. Birch Chapel was built about 1596. It originally served as a private chapel for the Birch family, who lived at Birch Hall, where Manchester Grammar School is today. The chapel was a simple brick building with a stone slab roof, and it seated 350 people.

Everything looks very peaceful in this picture, but feelings used to run high in the little chapel, as Conformists and Non-Conformists battled for supremacy in the pulpit. George Birch disapproved strongly of the non-conformist minister (Henry Finch), and when George inherited the Birch estates he deprived Finch of the living of Birch in 1697. Finch and his followers then built Platt Chapel. This departure did not upset the growth of Birch Chapel, and in 1753 John Dickenson, of another prominent Rusholme family, gave the money for a small chapel, to be known as the Dickenson Chapel, to be added to the main building.

By 1844 the chapel was so crowded that a decision was taken to build a new church, and in 1846 the present St. James Church was opened. The total cost was £4,300; the Rev. George Henry Greville Anson gave £2,000, and the rest was raised by public subscription. This new church is not quite on the same site as the chapel, being approximately 20 yards to the east. It is interesting to note that the new church had 400 free sittings in the centre, the best section of the church, whilst the paid seats were in the side sections.

St. James closed for worship in 1979 and was purchased for conversion to a domestic dwelling; and although the interior has been considerable altered to suit its new role, the building itself will remain as the centrepiece of one of the prettiest areas of Rusholme.

St. James Church of England Brass Band, 1897

This photograph shows the St. James Brass Band in front of the old Rectory, which is now in the grounds of Manchester Grammar School.

"Little Birch", (Birch Infants' School), Dickenson Road, 1921 *left*

This photograph shows some of the children who attended "Little Birch" in 1921. On the right is Miss Elizabeth Hannah Woodhead, the headmistress, with the assistant teacher, Miss Patman, on the left. At the extreme right is Councillor W. F. Lane-Scott, who may have held a position similar to that of school governor. The photograph is particularly interesting as it is much less formal than the usual school photograph. All the children are holding toys; apparently they were invited to bring their favourite toy to school on that day for the photograph, and two children are sitting on the teachers' knees. Looking at this photograph, one feels that "Little Birch" Infants must be a happy memory for many people.

The school was in Dickenson Road, almost opposite Stanley Avenue, on a site now occupied by Council houses. It says something for the density of traffic in Dickenson Road over 60 years ago, that the children could be grouped in the road – and the photographer, with his camera on tripod, could be in the middle of the road – on a weekday, without danger to life and limb.

Birch School, or "Big Birch", Danes Road, c.1976; prior to demolition *below left*

Another Birch connection – Birch School. As the date stone shows, the school was opened in 1841, a few years before the consecration of St. James Church. It stood to the south of the church, roughly on the site of the recent housing development. When it was built, the Gore Brook flowed in a wide bend past the front of the school, but this bend was removed when the footbridge over the brook was replaced by the present bridge.

This photograph shows the school, badly vandalized and overgrown, shortly before its demolition, about 1976. The new school – St. James Church of England Primary School – was opened in 1965, when Birch School closed, although the old building was used by Hollings College for some years, and, in the 1970's, there were proposals to convert it into four dwellings.

Buckley writes of an earlier school situated at the corner of Birch Hall Lane and Dickenson Road. It was a long, low building with diamond-shaped window panes and was known as "Chadwick's School", Chadwick being the teacher. This school was used both as a Day School and a Sunday School, and on Sundays the scholars marched in procession down Birch Hall Lane to Birch Chapel for services. On a sunny morning it must have made a pretty picture – a parade of children in their Sunday best, walking along what then would have been a country lane.

When Birch School opened in 1841, Chadwick's school was apparently kept on as an infants' school for a few years, until a new infants' school on Dickenson Road was opened in 1846 or 1850. (A little confusion here – Buckley says 5th August 1850, Royle says 1846.) Located opposite Stanley Avenue, on the site of new flats, this school was known as "Little Birch"; consequently Birch School became "Big Birch".

BIRCH SCHOOL
MDCCCXLI.

Birch Fold and Birch Hall Farm, November 1924

This series of pictures shows Old Hall Lane, and the farm land beyond it, as they were 60 years ago (on 21st November 1924). The top picture shows Old Hall Lane looking towards what is now Birchfields Road. Today, the Manchester Grammar School playing fields are on the left of the road, and No. 197 on the right. The track on the right leads to Birch Fold Farm, the outbuildings of which can be seen; and the track ahead, curving away to the left, leads to Birch Hall and Birch Hall Farm. The picture below right shows the scene, on the same track, approaching Birch Hall. This unusual view shows the outbuildings in the foreground, and the windows of the Victorian extensions in the background. The mediaeval black and white Hall is hidden behind the outbuildings. Birch Hall Farm can just be seen through the trees on the right.

Continuing past the Hall, the track leads to Birch Hall Farm, seen in the third picture (below), and finally out on to Birch Hall Lane.

Five generations of the Ratcliffe family farmed at Birch Hall Farm. When the farm was sold in 1926, the family moved to the Styal area where they have continued the farming tradition to the present day.

Birch Hall Farm

Birch Hall, Birch Hall Lane, c.1920

The earliest deed known to mention the Birch estate is dated 1190, when the property passed to Matthew de Birches. At that time, part of the estate consisted of woods – in which swine were allowed to feed – and a large mill for the grinding of corn. The mill would be water-powered at a time when the flow of water in the Brook would be substantially greater than it is today, now that much of the surface drainage water has been diverted into the sewers. There was a weir on the Brook in Birchfields as late as the 19th century.

The Hall remained in the Birch family until 1743, when it was sold, together with 168 acres of land, to John Dickenson for £6,000. During the 18th and 19th centuries it was altered and added to, until the old black and white Hall was almost hidden by the additions. In 1926 it was again sold, and the Hall and Farm buildings demolished. The Hall timbers were individually numbered, and it was rumoured that they had been sold to an American and that the Hall would be rebuilt in the United States. This scheme must have fallen through, however, because the Manchester Evening News then opened an appeal for funds with which to purchase the timbers for use in the repair of Warburton Old Church. That appeal was successful, and the timbers eventually went to Warburton.

In 1931 the buildings of Manchester Grammar School were erected on the site, and all traces of Birch Hall and Farm disappeared.

Birch Fold Cottage, Old Hall Lane, c.1905

This cottage was reached from the drive to Birch Hall Farm, which left Old Hall Lane between the present site of nos. 161 and 197. The thatched cottage was said to have been the oldest house in Rusholme, when it was demolished in 1912.

William Royle says, in his book "History of Rusholme", published in 1914, that "there are some of us left who remember distinct traces of it having been surrounded by a moat. I remember in my young days that this house was pointed to us as the one where Oliver Cromwell once slept".

Old Hall Lane, January 1941 *below*

The first six of these houses were damaged by blast from a large bomb which fell in the grounds of Manchester Grammar School, on the opposite side of the road. Fortunately, the playing fields are several feet below pavement level, so that the blast was diverted upwards, resulting in considerable damage to roofs, doors and windows, but little structural damage, and no casualties among the occupiers. Repair of the houses did not commence until 1947, because nearly all building materials and labour were directed towards maintaining the war effort in the years between.

The track on the right of the picture leads to Birch Fold Cottage, the chimney stack and gable end of which can be seen through the hedge. The Cottage has since been demolished.

Exhibition Hall, Old Hall Lane, 8th December 1913 *inset*

"£11,000 fire, to welcome Mr. Asquith" said the Daily Dispatch, in printing this picture of the scene at the corner of Old Hall Lane and Whitworth Lane (now a corner of the Manchester Grammar School playing fields). Built five years ago , the paper went on, at a cost of £11,000, the hall was the biggest of its kind in the country, excluding London's Olympia. It was 600 feet long by 216 feet wide, and had a ground floor capacity of 100,000 square feet. The belief that the fire was the work of suffragists, was later confirmed by the finding of a message for Mr. Asquith containing the words "This is your welcome to Manchester and Oldham".

Birch Hall Lane (junction with Telfer Road) c.1925 *above*

The land in the immediate foreground is now an entrance to Manchester Grammar School. Beyond the railings, on the left, is the south-eastern corner of Birchfields Park, and on the right, the then new houses of Birch Hall Lane. But the real interest in this photograph lies in the two large gateposts. To understand what these are and why they are here, we must go back to 1745, when John Dickenson – a Manchester merchant – lived in "Mr. Dickenson's House" on Market Stead Lane (now Market Street, in the City Centre). In that year, and in that house, John Dickenson entertained Bonnie Prince Charlie on his way south. In the same year, John Dickenson bought Birch Hall and went to live there. "The bed on which the Pretender lay" was moved by Dickenson to Birch Hall, and so, eventually, were the two gateposts from the front of the Market Street house. These relics of the late 17th century were at Birch until the Grammar School bought the land in 1926 and redeveloped the site, when they were probably destroyed.

"Finglands", Wilmslow Road, opposite Platt Lane, c.1950 *left*

This was the right-hand house of the pair of large houses known as Platt Terrace and was the last to be demolished of the series of large houses – Platt Terrace, Platt Cottage, Platt House and Platt Abbey – which occupied the east side of Wilmslow Road between Birch Villa and Norman Road.

Wilmslow Road near Dickenson Road corner, 1950's *below left*

A wall of advertisements can bring back memories. Many of these could be found elsewhere in England during the 1950's, but some are particularly Mancunian, The Hippodrome and Opera House for example. The hoardings hide another defunct Manchester theatre, Leslie's Pavilion. At the time this photograph was taken, it was no longer used as a theatre, and the building itself was demolished in the 1970's. Birch Villa hotel is on the left. The Lambretta scooter might also bring back memories.

Platt Abbey, Wilmslow Road before 1950 *below*

Platt Abbey was demolished in 1950, together with Platt Cottage and Platt House, to make way for the blocks of flats seen there today. An old gatepost has been left by the Wilmslow Road footpath and it bears the name Platt Cottage.

The novelist and playwright Ian Hay – real name John Hay Beith – was born at Platt Abbey in 1876, and a blue commemorative plaque notes this fact today. This photograph appears to have been taken on a warm sunny day; note the open windows and the deckchair on the lawn. In spite of its name, Platt Abbey was never an ecclesiastical foundation. Its Gothic-style windows may have inspired the name.

Brighton Grove gates on Wilmslow Road, c.1905 *above*

The Victorians had a penchant for rather grandiose housing schemes; consider Victoria Park, for example. The Brighton Grove Scheme with its palatial mansions, its gardens, bridges and lake, was one of these. However, it never really got much past the artist's impression stage; the company came to financial grief after only four houses had been commenced, and the plan was abandoned.

Today some of the original plan remains. One of the gateposts in the photograph can still be seen, and the style of the Liverpool Victoria Friendly Society suggests that it must have been one of the original buildings – it is almost identical with the first building on the left, in the artist's impression.

The lake was to have been formed by diverting and damming the Gore Brook at a time when the Brook was a clear, unpolluted stream. Even when Royle was young – in the 1860's – it was still pure, but industrial development upstream, in the Denton and Audenshaw area, soon caused a deterioration in the quality of the water, until it became as one sees and smells it today.

The 1841 Census showed Brighton Grove as having two lodges, both occupied by agricultural labourers and their families. There is probably no-one in Rusholme and Fallowfield today who could give "agricultural labourer" as their occupation, but in 1841 many people would have worked on the area's farms.

Melbourne House, Platt Lane, c.1905 *right*

Melbourne House on the right of this photograph, was named after Lord Melbourne, statesman and Prime Minister. It stood at the corner of Platt Lane and Wilmslow Road, and was demolished in the early 1920's to make way for the Rusholme Gardens block of flats. It is not known who the solemn-looking people staring at the camera are, or what the occasion was, but they also appear on another photograph of the period, with William Royle, at the gate of the former Platt School which was nearly opposite Melbourne House.

Holy Trinity Church, Platt Lane, 1902 *left*

Holy Trinity Church was consecrated in June 1846. Apparently there was some competition with the new Birch Church as to which would be ready first; Holy Trinity won, Birch being consecrated a week later, in July 1846. Mr. Thomas Carill-Worsley paid the cost of the building which was £5,600. There is an interesting story as to why Mr. Carill-Worsley was so generous. Returning to Rusholme after a long absence spent travelling in foreign parts, he found that Platt Chapel, where he and his family worshipped, had become unalterably Unitarian. He therefore decided to build a new church, and gave it the name Holy Trinity to ensure that it too, did not become Unitarian. Unfortunately, he died two years after the consecration, so did not have much time to enjoy the new church.

The architect was Mr. Edmund Sharpe, and he chose terracotta for his material. It was an unusual choice, and perhaps not a wise one, for large cracks and fissures developed in the graceful spire around 1910, and it had to be rebuilt. Today this replacement spire, which is a slightly different colour from the rest of the church, is one of the landmarks of Rusholme.

In 1902 the public spirited men of Holy Trinity met to plan celebrations for Rusholme's children, to usher in the Edwardian era. The photograph shows them all wearing medals, which probably were issued to commemorate the Coronation. Perhaps some Rusholme people have these medals in their possession today.

Holy Trinity Platt School, Grove Street, Rusholme, 1930 *above left*

This school was opened in 1861. Royle was one of its first pupils. Prior to its opening pupils had attended the Platt Day Schools in some since demolished outbuildings at the back of Platt Hall. The school closed in 1968, and today the building is known as the Trinity House Family Centre, where the Save the Children organisation runs a family support service and various community groups use the facilities.

Platt Lane Methodist Sunday School, 1937 *above right*

Our picture shows the head of the procession from Platt Lane Methodist Sunday School, as its members walked round part of its "parish". Mr. Hoole (with the Boys' Brigade lapel badges) checks the time; on his left, Mr. Herbert Cooper; and, in the foreground, watching us, is Mr. Alf Brown.

Platt Hall, 11th April 1910

Platt Hall is the site of one of the earliest of the recorded buildings of Rusholme, for until about 1764 a mediaeval black and white hall stood here. Both Platt and Birch Halls are mentioned in deeds of 1190.

Platt Hall came into the possession of the Platt family when it was transferred from the ownership of the Knights of St. John, and remained in the family's ownership until 1625, when it was sold to Ralph Worsley, a successful Manchester textile merchant who, before the days of the factories, supplied many of the inhabitants of Rusholme and Fallowfield with handlooms and yarn. He bought the finished cloth from them, storing some of it at Platt Hall and then removing it to his premises in Market Stead Lane (Market Street), Manchester.

Ralph's son, Charles, became involved in the Civil War, fighting on the Parliament side and rising to the rank of Major General. He was the man who, on the command of Cromwell to "take away that bauble", removed the Mace from the House of Commons, and kept it safely until the next Parliament assembled. His death at the early age of 34 robbed Rusholme, and the country, of a most able administrator and conciliator, at a time when both were sorely needed. Worsleys and Carrill-Worsleys continued to own Platt Hall until the early years of the century, when the whole Estate came on the market.

The story from this point is taken up on page 33.

Haymaking at Demesne Farm, Platt, c.1905

The land cultivated by the farmer at Demesne Farm – which was near to today's junction of Platt Lane and Yew Tree Road – stretched as far as Wilmslow Road, and to the private garden in front of Platt Hall. The lodge on Wilmslow Road, almost opposite Norman Road, is just off the right-hand edge of the picture, and the spire of Rusholme Congregational Church, Wilmslow Road, to the left of the large beech trees. The last of the great beech trees, which must have been familiar to a dozen generations of the Worsley family, were cut down in 1983.

In the days before the introduction of mechanisation to the agricultural scene, haymaking was one of the times when the whole family could help.

Desmesne Farm

31

William Royle and some Rusholme children

Royle vowed to save Platt Fields for the children of Rusholme. Certainly some of them in this picture with Royle look as if they could do with a little fresh air and sunshine. The decorated hoop held by one of the children suggests that this gathering was probably part of Rusholme's May Day celebrations.

The beginnings of Platt Fields lake, prior to 1910 *below*

Royle's dream takes shape; no massive earth moving machines in sight, just men, horses, and carts. There was considerable unemployment during the winter of 1908/9, and many of the unemployed took jobs on the Platt Fields project. The men constructed an impressive lake which covered 6½ acres. Work was finished before the official opening took place,

Opening of Platt Fields Park, 7th May 1910

The Platt Estate, comprising the Hall, its immediate grounds, and about 80 acres of agricultural land were offered for sale by auction in 1901 and again in 1906 but in neither case was the reserve price reached, so the owners decided to sell the Estate piecemeal, and, in 1907, sold the Hall, and land fronting Wilmslow Road and Platt Lane. The purchaser intended to pull the Hall down, and use the bricks to build shops fronting the roads. Many appeals had been made to the Corporation and to certain "very wealthy citizens", but all in vain.

At this stage William Royle became involved. He managed to talk the purchaser into agreeing to resell the Hall and nearby land at his own purchase price. He flooded Rusholme with circulars exhorting Rusholme citizens to take an interest in the future of Platt "Fields", as he now called it. He persuaded the Lord Mayor to call a Town's Meeting – even though the requisite number of citizens had not requested it – and then packed it with Rusholmites. The Town's Meeting, naturally, passed a resolution recommending the City Council to buy the Platt Estate for use as a public park, and this the Council ultimately did, at a cost of nearly £60,000. Platt Fields Park was formally opened by the Lord Mayor (Councillor Behrens) on 7th May 1910, and our picture shows William Royle addressing the crowd.

Opening Day, on the lake

It was a splendid occasion; the Lord Mayor, Councillor Behrens, wore his chain of office, and most of the men wore top hats except Royle – seated third from the end looking directly at the camera – who wore a more modest bowler. The photograph was taken from the Boat house, looking towards Platt Lane, with the spire of Holy Trinity showing above the young trees. Public occasions like this attracted thousands of orderly spectators, for whom the opening of this imaginatively-designed Park was a very special occasion.

The Band, Platt Fields, Manchester.

Tank in Platt Fields, 5th May 1919 *inset*

In May 1919, the war had been over for six months, so that the reason for the presence of this tank in Platt Fields would hardly be a recruiting drive. Perhaps it was the army's way of saying thankyou to the local population for the effort which they put into waging the war.

Platt Fields bandstand, about 1930 *left*

Until the 1960's the bandstand stood in the centre of a tiered, circular enclosure near the Grangethorpe Road entrance. When it was demolished, the enclosure was filled in to the level of the surrounding ground, so that now there is very little to indicate its whereabouts.

The distant trees are along the line of Wilmslow Road, and they almost hide the old house (just to the right of the ticket booth) which was replaced by Appleby Lodge flats in the mid 1930's. Above the trees can just be seen the top of the spire of St. James, Birch.

Grangethorpe *right*

Grangethorpe was built about 1882 as a family mansion for one of the wealthy families coming into this area. It was an imposing house, richly decorated and heavily gabled, and set in large ornamental gardens. In 1916 it was sold to the British Red Cross, and was used as a hospital for the thousands of men wounded in Flanders, Gallipoli and the Somme. In 1929 the Ministry of Pensions closed the hospital as most of the injured no longer needed hospital treatment. It was sold to the Royal Infirmary, who in turn sold it to the Manchester High School for Girls in 1936.

Grangethorpe was demolished, and a new school building erected on the site. The girls moved into the school in September 1940 and, barely three months later, the school was totally destroyed by a German land mine dropped on December 23rd 1940. The school was rebuilt and opened again in 1951.

34

Cathedral masonry

Ashfield

Nico Ditch

The Nico Ditch is an earthwork which stretched from Ashton Moss (Ashton-under-Lyne) to Hough Moss (Chorlton), though only small sections are still visible in this area. Its line follows Old Hall Lane, Park Grove (Levenshulme/Rusholme boundary), and Matthews Lane (Levenshulme/Gorton boundary), and though for most of its distance it was a township boundary, it was originally a defensive earthwork, probably dating back to the 9th century, when Manchester was over-run by the Danes. The tradition is that it was dug in one night, each man digging a length equivalent to his own height, and this is probably an indication that the population would receive very short notice of an attack by the Danes, and would need to erect a strong defence with great speed. Similar defensive earthworks, but independent of this one, were constructed at about this time, to the east and south east of Manchester.

The picture shows the Nico Ditch where it forms the boundary between the Manchester High School for Girls and the Ashfield section of Platt Fields Park. Wilmslow Road follows the line of the wall across the picture, and Old Hall Lane continues the line of the Nico Ditch on the far side of Wilmslow Road. The building seen through the trees, behind the chestnut paling, is Platt Chapel.

The house known as Ashfield, dated back to about 1835. Its first owner was Mr. Robinson, "a well-known Manchester merchant" according to Royle, who adds that he was told by an old man, formerly gardener to Mr. Robinson, how "more than once or twice" foxes had run into the Ashfield gardens and been unable to escape from the hounds and huntsmen. Later on in the nineteenth century, the "extensive pleasure grounds still contained plantations, fish ponds and every kind of garden", according to Mrs. Williamson.

A special feature of the gardens was the group of fifteenth century windows from Manchester Cathedral, sold by the Cathedral authorities when the stonework of the nave was being replaced in the nineteenth century. Royle says that the old masonry was erected, first "at Manley Hall, the residence of Mr. Sam Mendel, but, over forty years ago" (i.e. about 1870), brought to and re-erected at Ashfield.

Our second picture shows, on the extreme left, the wall of what is now the Shakespearean garden, then the two clerestory windows with parapet above, and finally a complex of window cases, said to be from the north choir aisle.

Ashfield was bought by Manchester Corporation in 1913, the house and stables demolished, and the grounds added to Platt Fields. Maintenance of the former Cathedral masonry, was insufficient to prevent the collapse of the clerestory windows, and the stone was disposed of. Only the window case still survives in a corner of the Ashfield section of Platt Fields, near to the Nico Ditch.

Nico Ditch

Platt Chapel, Wilmslow Road, 1860's

This is how Platt Chapel looked before it was altered in the 1880's, when the walls were raised by about eighteen inches, and the present more steeply pitched roof added. Apparently these alterations were made to accommodate a gallery at the south end of the chapel. The bell tower was moved from the north to the south end, and the door facing Wilmslow Road moved to the south side.

The history of the Chapel is linked with the struggle between the conformists and non-conformists at Birch Chapel. In 1697 George Birch deprived the non-conformist minister, Henry Finch, of the living of Birch, forcing him and his loyal congregation to hold meetings in local houses. The situation was unsatisfactory, and at a meeting held in 1699, it was decided to build a new chapel. Mr. Raphe Worsley gave the site, a section of the area known as Blake Flatt, and the first Platt Chapel was built in 1700 at a cost, including furnishings, of £95, Mr. Finch and Mr. Worsley providing a third of the money. Mr. Finch was the first minister of the newly built chapel, and when he died in 1704, non-conformism had become well-established. By 1714, the congregation had grown to 250, although they must have been crowded as the seating plan of 1700 showed places for only 128! A new chapel was built on this site in 1790/1, although the reasons for the demolition and re-building are not known.

In 1970 this chapel, which had served Rusholme for so long, was closed for worship; like so many other churches in the area, congregations had dwindled to a point where it was impossible to maintain the building. The Chapel registers of baptisms, marriages and deaths, have been deposited in the Local History Library in Manchester's Central Library, where they may be inspected.

As Platt Chapel is a Grade II listed building, i.e. of architectural or historic interest, the possibility that it would be vandalised whilst it remained empty caused some anxiety in the community, but, fortunately, it was purchased by the Manchester Amateur Photographic Society, and is now well maintained. It stands as a reminder of those stormy ecclesiastical times when Rusholme was almost wholly agricultural.

Royle tells a gruesome tale of an incident which occurred in the graveyard of Platt Chapel in 1833. Apparently the village nightwatchman discovered a group of body snatchers raiding one of the graves. Upon being disturbed they fled, leaving the corpse beside the grave. The children who attended the Sunday School at Platt Chapel were so frightened by this event, that they all switched their religious allegiance to the Wesleyan Sunday School.

The photograph was taken before the arrival of the horse trams in 1880, and before tarmacadam was available to seal the surface of the road.

The Oaks Lodge, corner of old Hall Lane and Wilmslow Road, 1907

This is the original lodge of The Oaks, now Ashburne Hall. It was demolished during the 1920's, and the present lodge was built further back on the site. The street sign for Old Hall Lane can just be seen on the left.

The Oaks was built between 1835 and 1838 for Robert Ogden who owned a cotton spinning mill, Shepley Street Mill, near London Road Fire Station. Ogden also owned a public house, the Ogden Arms at the corner of Richmond Street and Canal Street, conveniently close to his factory.

He died in 1848. His sons continued with the business, and each of his daughters inherited £10,000, a considerable sum in those days.

The 1841 Census gives further information on the size of Robert and Caroline Ogden's establishment. There were four daughters – Harriet, Elizabeth, Amilia and Caroline, and three sons – Thomas, Charles and Frederick. They had 6 female servants, one male servant and a coachman. By comparison today Ashburne Hall houses about 200 students.

The house was bought by Edward Behrens sometime after 1869, and it became a university hall of residence around 1926. Not to be confused with the Ashburne House at the corner of Conyngham Road and Oxford Place, which was the original home of this hall of residence.

"Wilbraham Road extension" (Moseley Road), 1905 *right*

The picture shows the line of the road, after the wall of The Firs and of Firs Farm had been set back, leaving the trees inside the area allocated for the road. On the right is the new railing of Moseley Road School, and beyond that, the shop and houses at the corner of Balmoral Road.

Wilmslow Road, corner of Oak Drive, c.1908

Oak Drive was a U-shaped road, having two junctions with Wilmslow Road. This picture shows the northern arms of Oak Drive, almost opposite Mabfield Road. A section of the roadway of Oak Drive is still to be seen inside Owens Park grounds.

Oak House, shown here, was a typical product of the 1830–1840 period. Its front elevation resembles that of "Mr. Hadfield's house" in Conyngham Road, Victoria Park, which was built in 1837, and which still stands. Garden walls were high round the big houses, mainly to maintain the privacy of the family when in the garden, although this object must have been defeated with the advent of the double-decker electric tram, which here dwarfs the cab and the commercial lorry. This series of car was ordered with open tops, but while they were being built, the Tramways committee had a change of heart, and decided that at least the seating area upstairs should be covered and enclosed. It was 1926 before the ends were enclosed – driving must have been a nightmare in bad weather.

37

Cawdor Road, Fallowfield; Bomb damage, October 1940 *above left*

Another scene illustrating the problems which some of the war-time residents had to face. The crater shows that the bomb fell almost exactly in the middle of the road, and so, although it caused considerable damage to nearby houses none of them had to be demolished, and today it is not possible to tell that the houses were ever damaged. The street trees shown here have been replaced by smaller decorative varieties, whilst the house in Albion Road, facing the camera, is over-shadowed by a tree growing behind it. The gas lamps would not be lit during the war, and had a white band painted at about eye level so that they could be seen more easily in the black-out.

Corner of Wilmslow Road and Cawdor Road, c.1950 *above right*

The shop then occupied by Ellis & Sons on the corner of Cawdor Road is now an open space. In the late 1970's during the course of some alterations to the

building it completely collapsed. Various proposals have been put forward for rebuilding on the site, but the cost of rebuilding to the same design, with the same detailing, would be too great, and a simpler building would be out of place on the site. The solution was to turn it into a mini-park, with a seat and trees.

Barcombe Hotel (Waterhouse's Barcombe Cottage), January 10th 1941 *right*

This house was on the south arm of Oak Drive, close to Wilmslow Road and to the present day Oak House (Beech House) student flats. It was designed, built and occupied by Alfred Waterhouse (architect of Manchester Town Hall) before he was attracted to London by the promise of substantial commissions. At the time when this damage by high explosive bomb occurred it was a private house, and the owner has put out his largest flag to indicate to the world that he intends to be back in occupation as soon as possible. After the war, the building was repaired, and was used as an hotel until its demolition. The crater made by the bomb is in the left foreground.

Holy Innocents Church, Wilmslow Road, Fallowfield, early 1900's *below*

Holy Innocents was consecrated in 1872. When it opened the church had 706 sittings, of which 402 were free. This idea of paying for a pew seems very strange today, and must have divided congregations into rich and poor in a very un-Christian way. At the time this photograph was taken, Wilbraham Road was a private road, and the gates deterred the casual passer-by from entering. In 1954 Holy Innocents was damaged by a fire which caused thousands of pounds worth of damage. When St. James Church closed in 1979, the two parishes were united to form the parish of The Holy Innocents and St. James, Fallowfield.

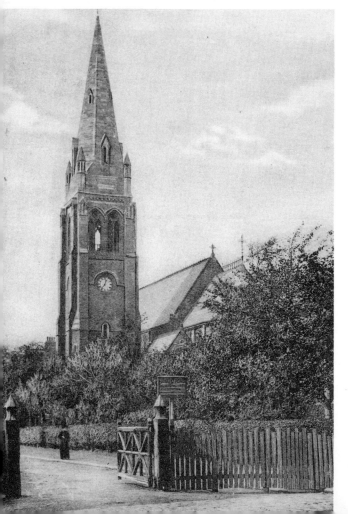

Manchester Athletic Club (MAC) ground, Whitworth Lane *above*

The MAC ground dates from about 1891, and was originally built for field games. In the early years of the 20th century, the banked cycle track was added, and cycle racing took place there for over fifty years. The Manchester racing cyclist, Reg Harris, bought the ground about 1955, renaming it the Harris Stadium. Cycle racing continued there until – and even after – the ground was bought by the University, but eventually with the building of the Owens Park complex, and the conversion of the land adjoining the track to a car park, racing ceased. The stadium is still complete, and is used for athletics by University students.

The photograph shows cycle racing at the Ground in about 1910. In the centre of the skyline can be seen the spire of Holy Innocents church at the corner of Wilbraham Road and Wilmslow Road, and to its right the 19th century houses on Oak Drive, which were demolished before the building of Owens Park commenced. Behind the stands on the left of the picture are some of the buildings of Firs farm, the only one of the farms of Rusholme and Fallowfield which can still be seen today, although not in use as a farm.

Friendship Inn, Wilmslow Road, 1920

Not to be confused with the present day Friendship Inn on the other side of Wilmslow Road, this Friendship Inn stood opposite Carill Drive until its demolition in the 1960's. The roof-line is much lower than that of its neighbours and this, together with the small windows, suggests that this row of houses was built around the beginning of the 1800's. Mrs. Williamson's book confirms this; in the section dealing with Fallowfield before 1830 she writes, "What is now the Friendship Inn was combined with the adjoining house to form a bakehouse and village store, and the only one between Withington and Rusholme".

Moseley Road School (Levenshulme High School, Lower School), Moseley Road, c.1916

Casualties during the 1914–1918 war were so great that many large buildings were pressed into use as military hospitals. Grangethorpe (where the Manchester High School for Girls now stands) was one of these, and the school shown in this picture was another.

The road in the foreground is the "new" section of Ladybarn Road, on the Levenshulme side of Ladybarn Lane. The old part of Ladybarn Road led to Small Oak and Large Oak Farms, which were close together on sites at the right-hand edge of this picture. They were demolished to allow the road seen here to be built.